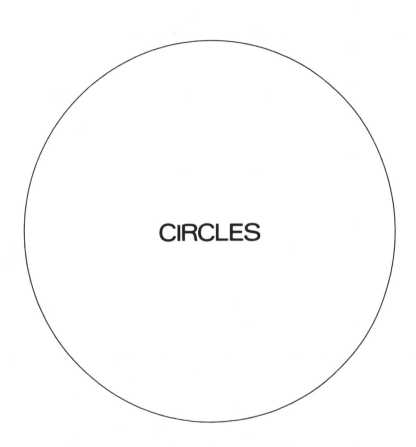

CIRCLES

$4.46

513
SIT

Sitomer, Mindel

Circles

CIRCLES

BY MINDEL
AND HARRY
SITOMER
ILLUSTRATED
BY GEORGE
GIUSTI

Thomas Y. Crowell Company New York

YOUNG MATH BOOKS

Edited by Dr. Max Beberman, Director of the Committee on School Mathematics Projects, University of Illinois

BIGGER AND SMALLER *by Robert Froman*

CIRCLES *by Mindel and Harry Sitomer*

COMPUTERS *by Jane Jonas Srivastava*

THE ELLIPSE *by Mannis Charosh*

ESTIMATION *by Charles F. Linn*

FRACTIONS ARE PARTS OF THINGS
by J. Richard Dennis

GRAPH GAMES *by Frédérique and Papy*

LINES, SEGMENTS, POLYGONS
by Mindel and Harry Sitomer

LONG, SHORT, HIGH, LOW, THIN, WIDE
by James T. Fey

MATHEMATICAL GAMES FOR ONE OR TWO
by Mannis Charosh

ODDS AND EVENS *by Thomas C. O'Brien*

PROBABILITY *by Charles F. Linn*

RIGHT ANGLES: PAPER-FOLDING GEOMETRY
by Jo Phillips

RUBBER BANDS, BASEBALLS AND DOUGHNUTS:
A BOOK ABOUT TOPOLOGY *by Robert Froman*

STRAIGHT LINES, PARALLEL LINES,
PERPENDICULAR LINES *by Mannis Charosh*

WEIGHING & BALANCING *by Jane Jonas Srivastava*

WHAT IS SYMMETRY? *by Mindel and Harry Sitomer*

Edited by Dorothy Bloomfield, Mathematics Specialist, Bank Street College of Education

AREA *by Jane Jonas Srivastava*

GAME OF FUNCTIONS *by Robert Froman*

LESS THAN NOTHING IS REALLY SOMETHING
by Robert Froman

NUMBER IDEAS THROUGH PICTURES
by Mannis Charosh

SHADOW GEOMETRY *by Daphne Harwood Trivett*

SPIRALS *by Mindel and Harry Sitomer*

STATISTICS *by Jane Jonas Srivastava*

VENN DIAGRAMS *by Robert Froman*

Manufactured in the United States of America
L.C. Card 71-113856
ISBN 0-690-19430-7
0-690-19431-5 (LB)
4   5   6   7   8   9   10

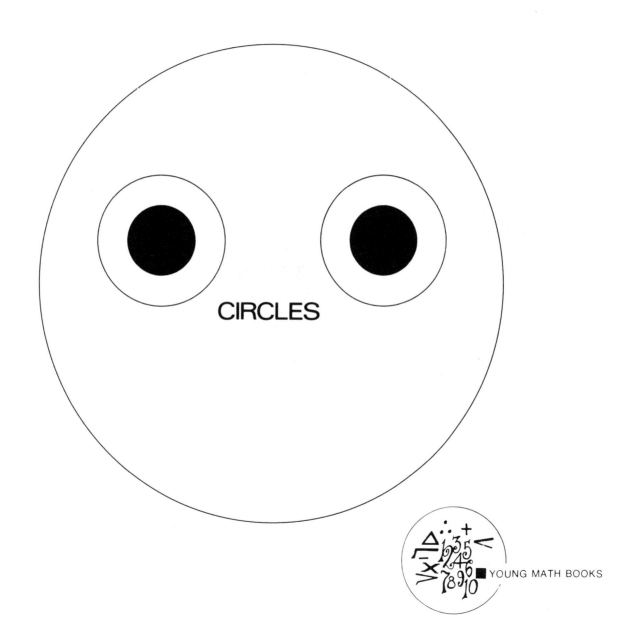

CIRCLES

YOUNG MATH BOOKS

Have you ever dropped a pebble into a still pond and watched the ripples? They start out as little circles and grow into big ones. All the circles have the same center. It is where the pebble fell into the water.

Have you ever played a game where you hold hands to form a circle? Sometimes someone stands at the center.

A circle has no corners.

Coins are made circular so that they don't tear your pockets.

Pots and pans are often made with circular bottoms. They are easier to clean if there are no corners that are hard to get into.

Most clocks have circular faces so that the hands can point clearly to the numerals. Did you ever try to read the time on a clock shaped like a rectangle? You have to be very careful to tell the difference between four o'clock and five o'clock.

There are circles all around you—in games, in machinery, and in nature.

A wheel, too, has the shape of a circle. The hub of the wheel is at the center. In many wheels the hub is connected to the rim by spokes.

It would be very odd if some of the spokes were longer than others. What kind of ride would you get with wheels like that?

In a good wheel all the spokes have the same length. That is why a wheel has the shape of a circle.

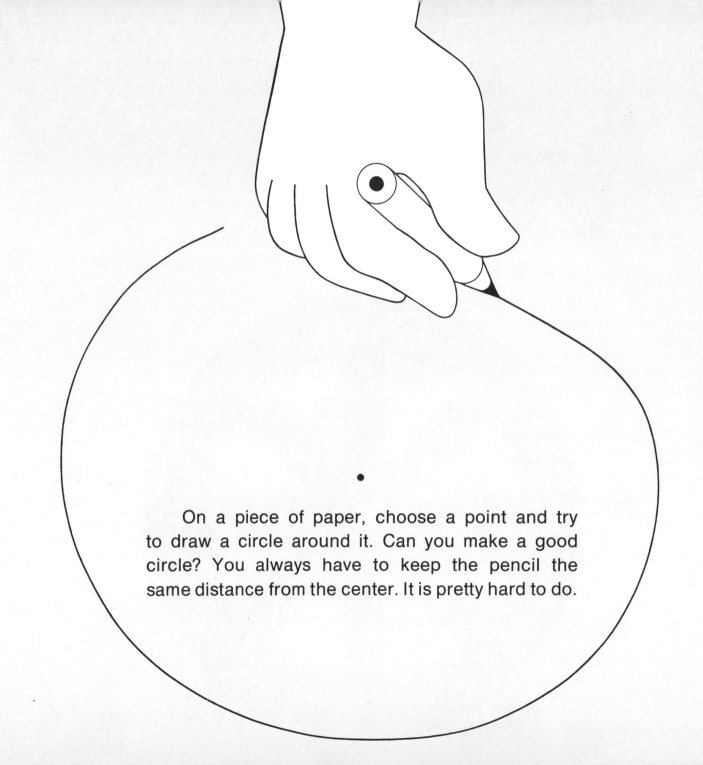

On a piece of paper, choose a point and try to draw a circle around it. Can you make a good circle? You always have to keep the pencil the same distance from the center. It is pretty hard to do.

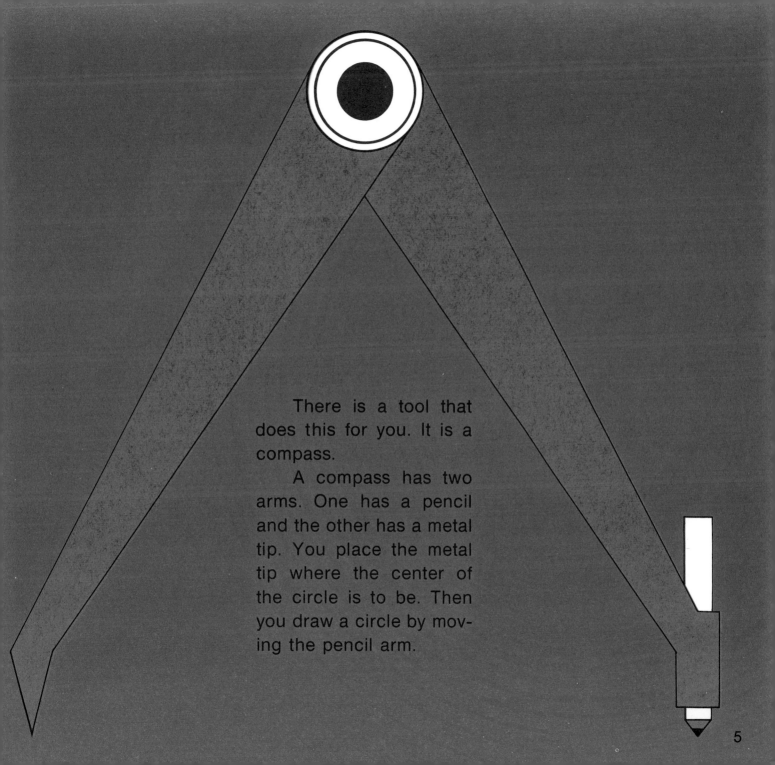

There is a tool that does this for you. It is a compass.

A compass has two arms. One has a pencil and the other has a metal tip. You place the metal tip where the center of the circle is to be. Then you draw a circle by moving the pencil arm.

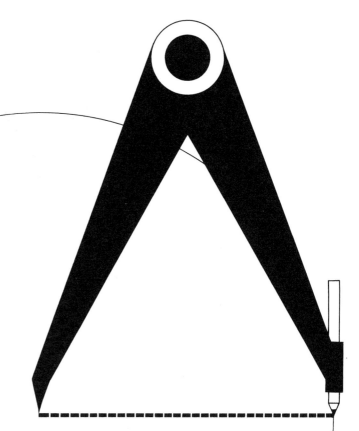

Remember that the metal tip is at the center of the circle. You can imagine line segments from the center to the pencil marks. They are like the spokes of a wheel. The compass keeps them all the same length. Each of these line segments is called a RADIUS. For more than one of them we say RADII.

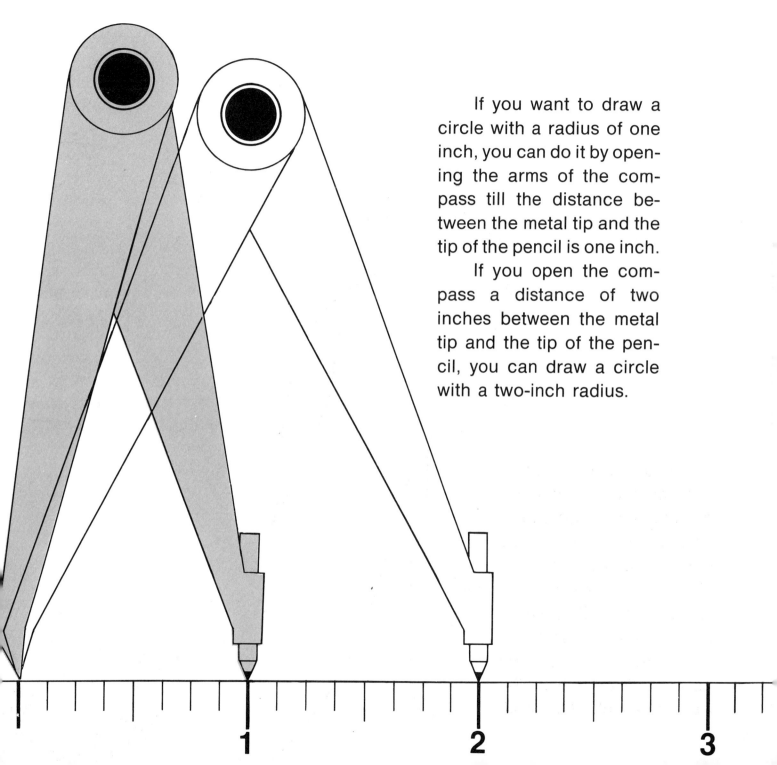

If you want to draw a circle with a radius of one inch, you can do it by opening the arms of the compass till the distance between the metal tip and the tip of the pencil is one inch.

If you open the compass a distance of two inches between the metal tip and the tip of the pencil, you can draw a circle with a two-inch radius.

1

2

3

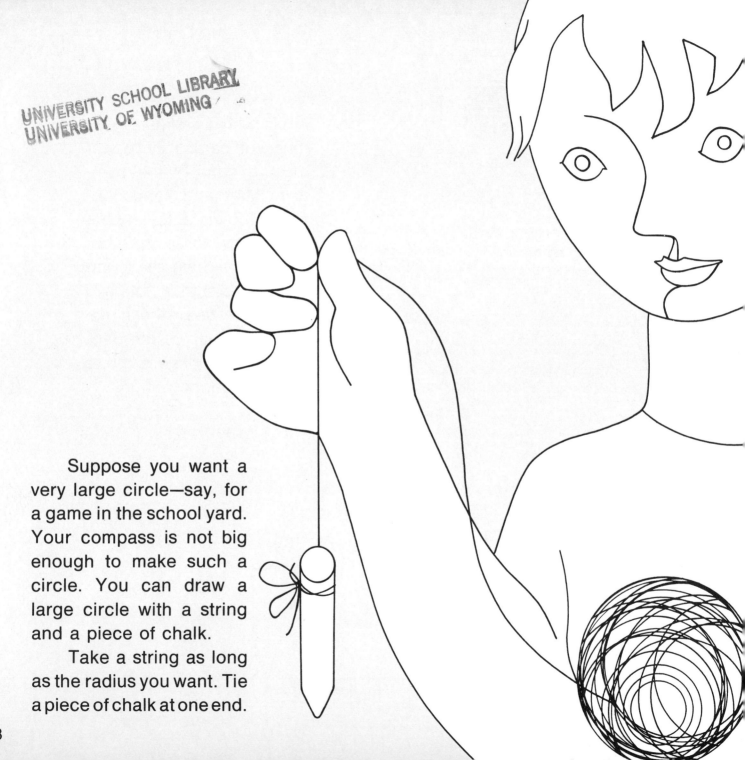

Suppose you want a very large circle—say, for a game in the school yard. Your compass is not big enough to make such a circle. You can draw a large circle with a string and a piece of chalk.

Take a string as long as the radius you want. Tie a piece of chalk at one end.

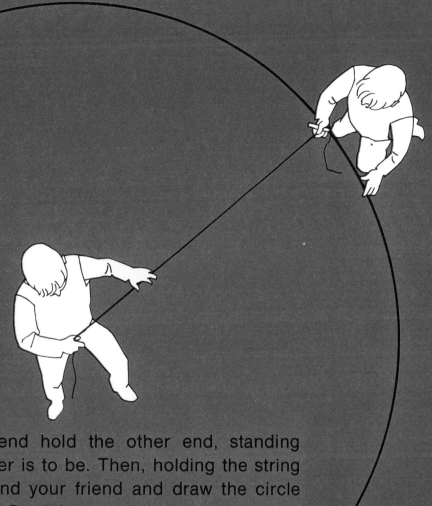

Have a friend hold the other end, standing where the center is to be. Then, holding the string taut, walk around your friend and draw the circle with your chalk. Don't let your friend get in the way of the string. As you walk, you are marking points that are all at the same distance from the center of the circle.

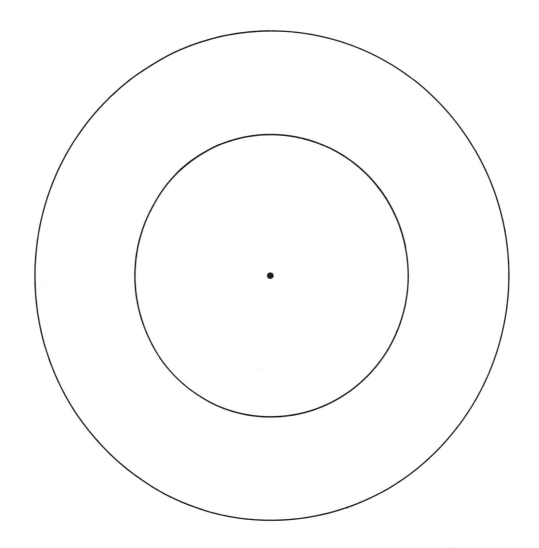

Here are some things to do with circles. On your paper, draw a small circle, using your compass. Now open the compass a little wider. With the same center, draw a larger circle. You now have two circles with the same center and different radii.

Can you draw still larger circles with the same center?

Can you draw two circles that touch each other? Can you draw a third circle that touches both of these circles? A line marked off in inches will help you.

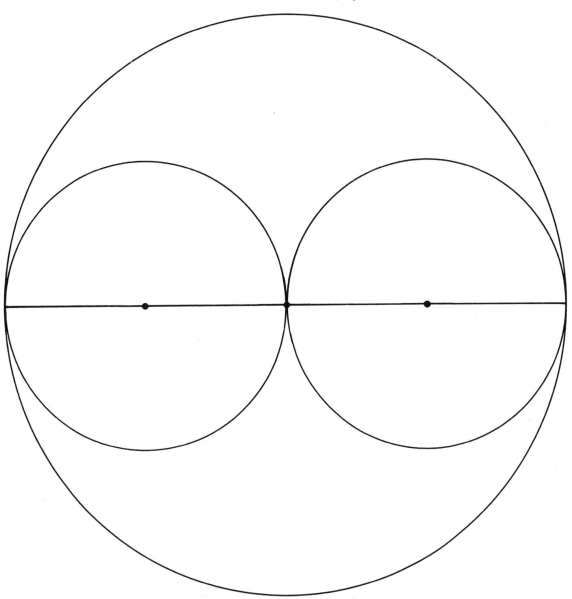

With your compass, draw a circle on your paper. From any point on the circle, draw a line segment through the center to another point on the circle. Such a line segment is called a DIAMETER of the circle. It is twice as long as the radius. As you can see, a diameter cuts its circle into two parts having the same shape and size. Each part is called a SEMICIRCLE. SEMI means half. So a semicircle is half a circle.

Now suppose you want to cut each semicircle in half. You can do this with a second diameter that makes square corners with the first. The picture shows how to place a sheet of paper with a square corner on the first diameter. Do you see how to draw the second diameter?

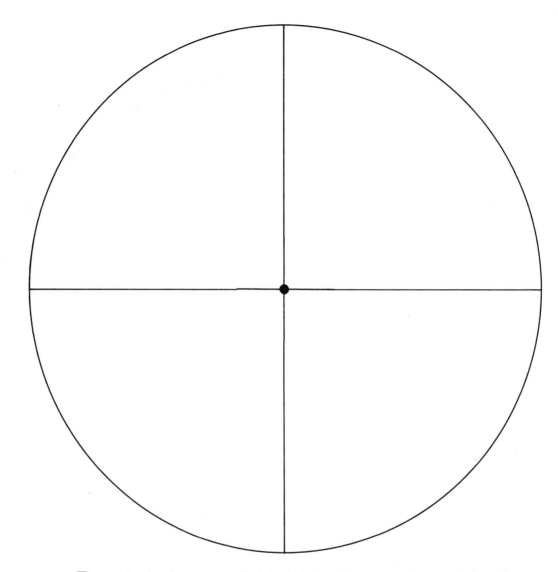

The circle is now divided into four parts. All the four parts have the same shape and size. Draw four line segments with a ruler to connect the four ends of the diameters. What shape have you made?

If you said a SQUARE, you can test to see if you are right. Each of the corners should be a square corner and

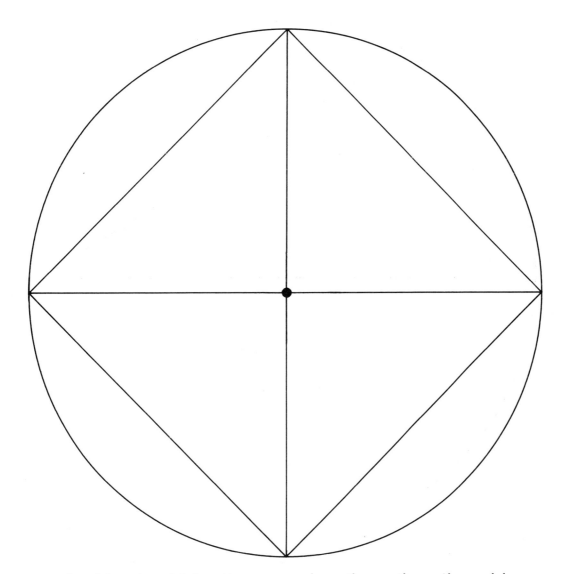

each side should be the same length as the other sides.

To make the square, you started by drawing two diameters. They divide the circle into four parts having the same shape and size. Can you draw four diameters to divide the circle into eight parts having the same shape and size?

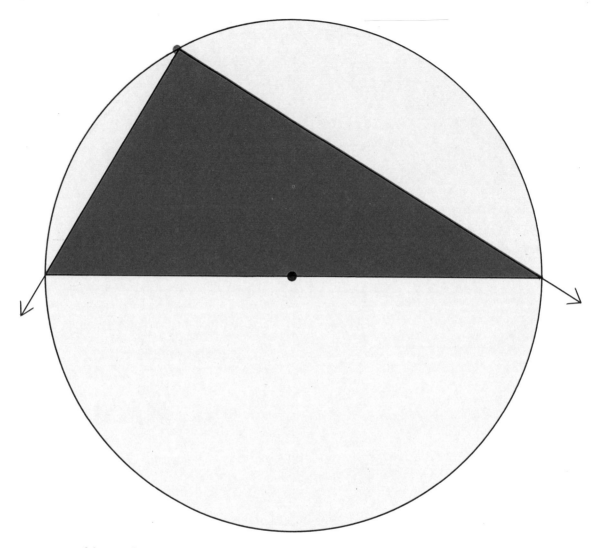

Here is an experiment. On your paper, draw a circle and one of its diameters. Then choose any point on one of the semicircles. We chose the red point. From this point draw a ray through one end of the diameter, and another ray through the other end. These two rays make an ANGLE. Now comes the interesting part. Try to fit the square corner of a sheet of paper into this angle. Does it fit, exactly?

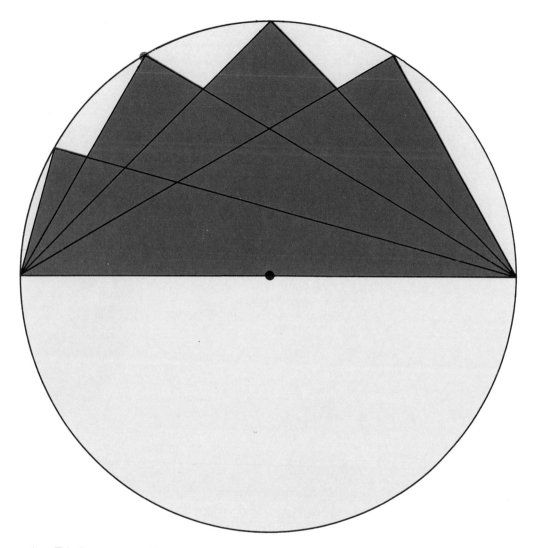

Pick any other point on one of the semicircles and draw the two rays. Have you drawn another square-corner angle? Try circles of different sizes. Try different points on the semicircles. Do you always get a square corner?

It doesn't matter how big or small the circle is. It doesn't matter which point you choose. You will always get square corners.

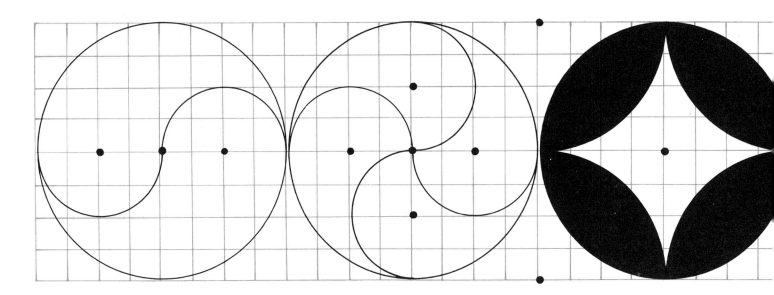

Here are some designs that use circles and parts of circles. You may have fun copying them. The centers of all circles or parts of circles are shown. You can tell the radius of each circle by counting the number of spaces on squared paper. The designs will be easier to copy, too, if you use squared paper.

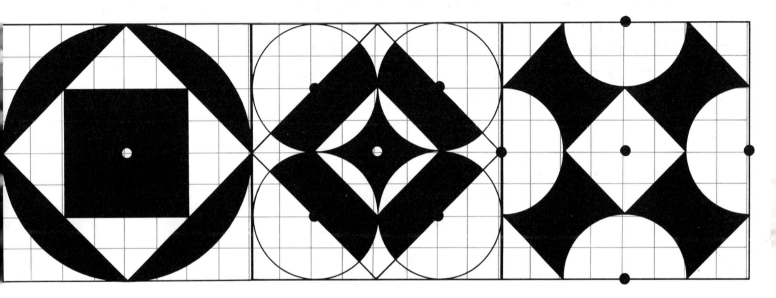

In the next set of designs there are both circles and squares. These are a little harder to copy. Study each design and find the center of each circle or part of a circle. Look for the squares.

Can you make your own circle-and-square designs?

Here is another experiment. First, make sure your pencil is sharp. Then draw a circle with your compass. It can be any size. Our circle has a two-inch radius.

Without changing your compass opening, set the metal tip at any point on the circle. In the picture that point is shown by the red dot. Cross the circle with the pencil. The black dot in the picture shows the place where the pencil crossed the circle.

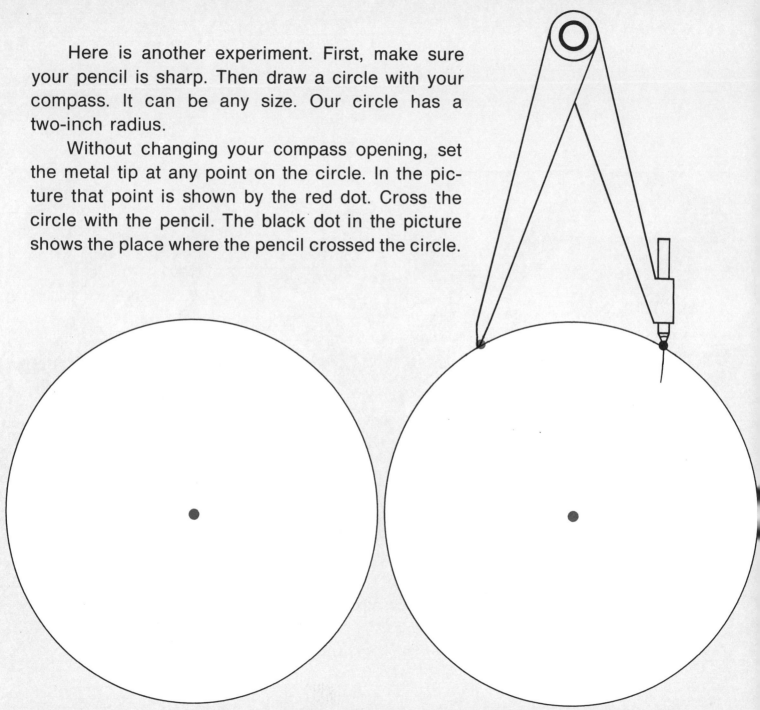

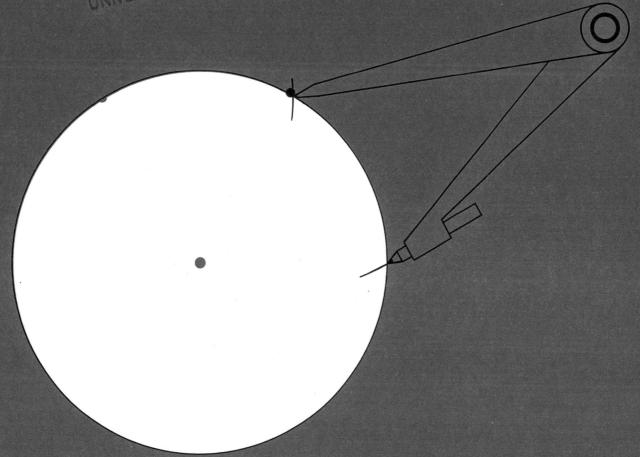

Now move the metal tip to the black dot and cross the circle with the pencil again. Keep this up. If you fix the metal tip carefully each time, you will find that the sixth crossing cuts the circle at the point where you started.

21

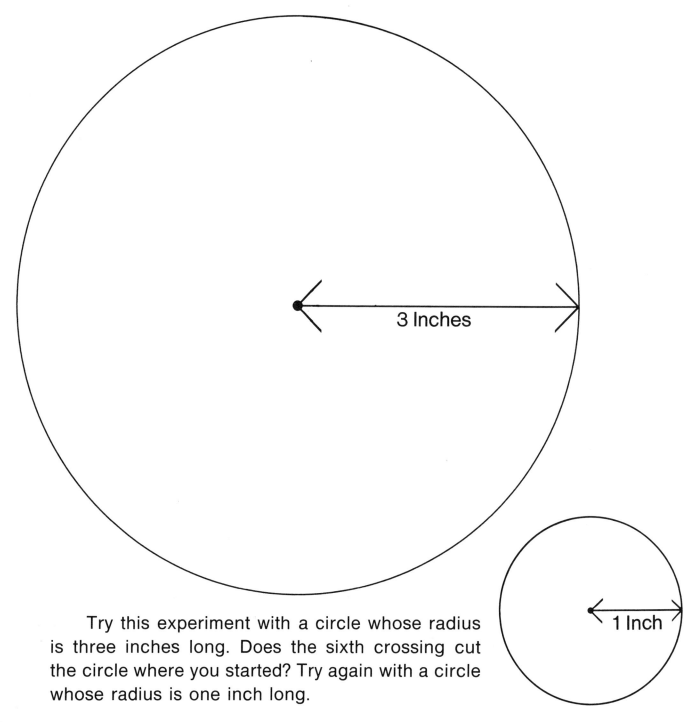

3 Inches

1 Inch

Try this experiment with a circle whose radius is three inches long. Does the sixth crossing cut the circle where you started? Try again with a circle whose radius is one inch long.

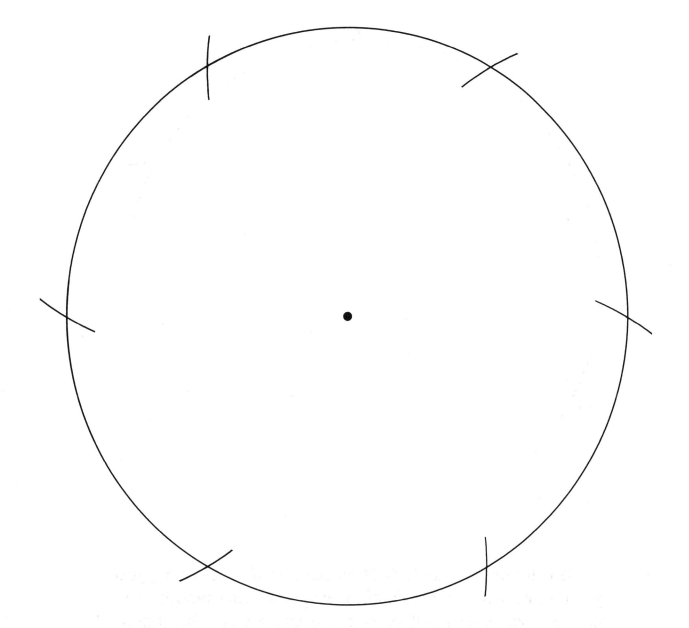

This way you can divide a circle into six parts, each having the same shape and size. We call the points that divide the circle DIVISION POINTS.

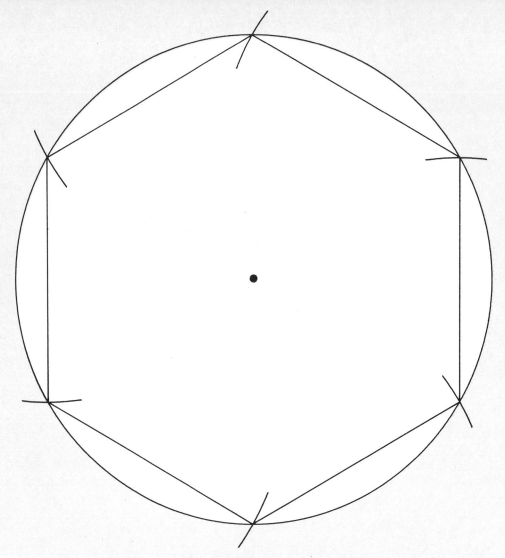

If you connect each division point to the next one, you get a figure with six sides, all having the same length. You also get six angles, all having the same size. Any figure that has six sides is called a HEXAGON. Whenever its sides have the same length and its angles have the same size, it is called REGULAR.

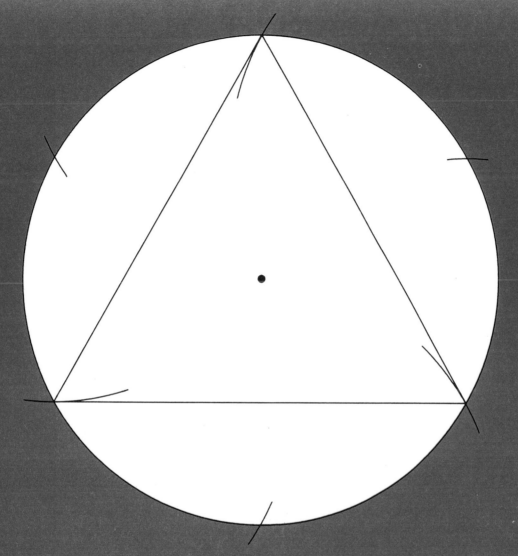

If you skip every other point and connect only three division points, you will get a TRIANGLE that is also regular. The three sides of this triangle have the same length, and its three angles have the same size.

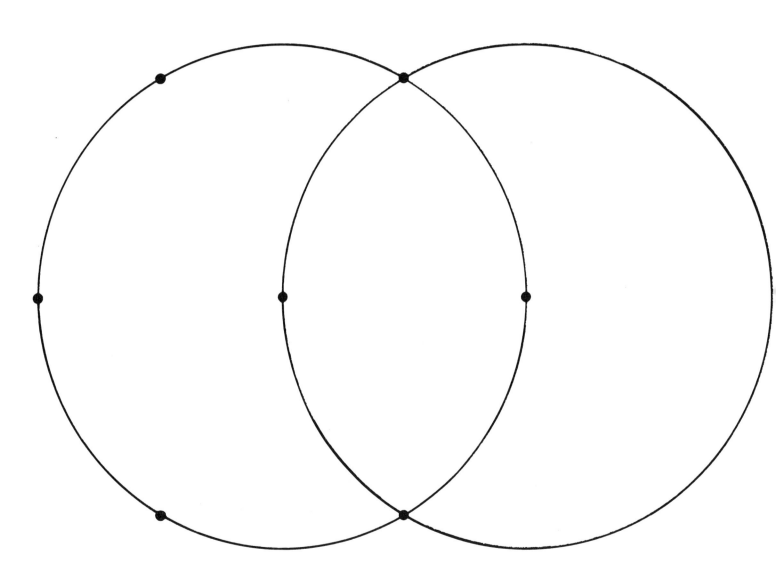

26

Now try another experiment. Divide a circle into six parts having the same size. Keep the same compass opening, and place the metal tip at one of the six division points. Now draw a circle.

Does the second circle pass through the center of the first circle? Does it also pass through two division points?

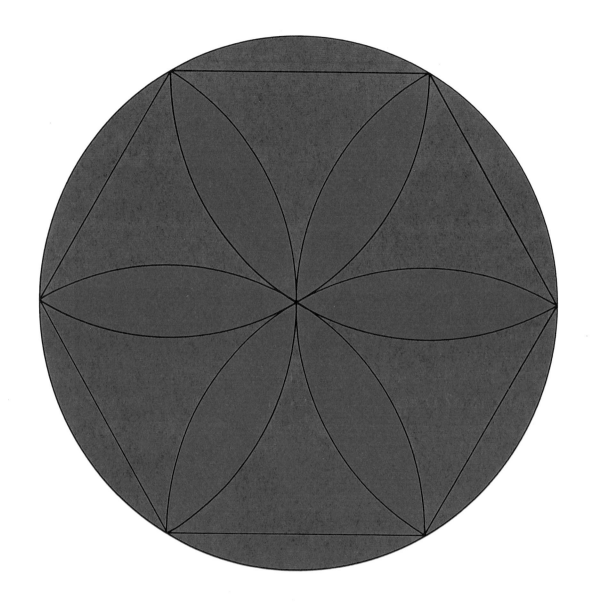

Here are more circle designs. Can you find the centers
of the circles? In each design, try to find six division points.
Try to find regular triangles and hexagons.

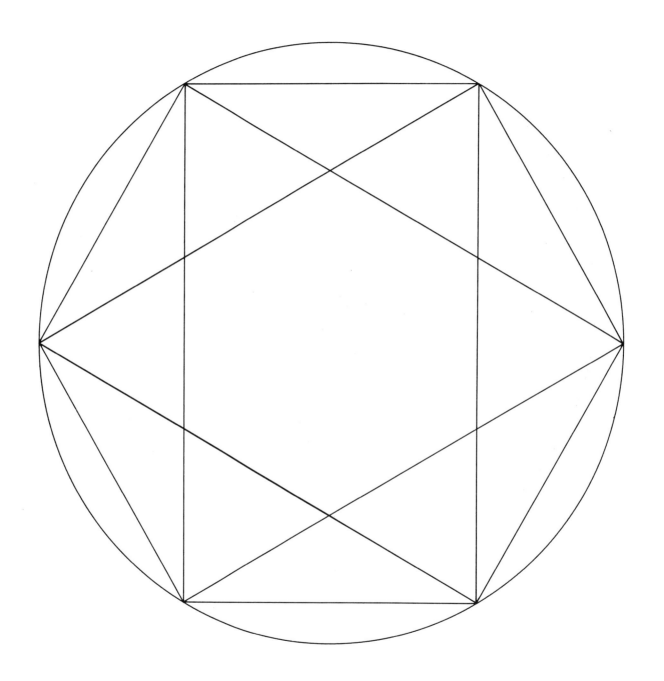

Can you find eight regular triangles and two regular hexagons in this design?

Can you also find three rectangles and twenty-four triangles that are not regular? Turn the page for the solution.

A long time ago, a man said, "The circle is the most perfect figure." Do you agree?

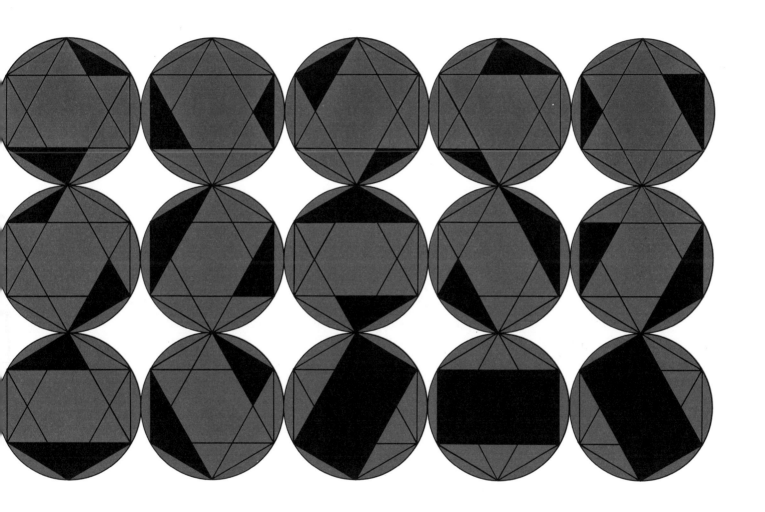

ABOUT THE AUTHORS

CIRCLES is the second book on which Mr. and Mrs. Sitomer have collaborated. Harry Sitomer was born in Russia and was educated in New York City. He has taught mathematics in both high school and college and is the coauthor of several mathematics textbooks. CIRCLES reflects Mr. Sitomer's interest and active participation in the current changes in school mathematics.

Mindel Sitomer was born and educated in New York City. She studied biology in college, and says that when her own children were small she learned that young people easily understand and enjoy hearing about major scientific concepts. That is one of the reasons she enjoyed working with her husband to present this information to young readers.

The Sitomers now live in Huntington, New York. They have two children and seven grandchildren.

ABOUT THE ILLUSTRATOR

George Giusti has illustrated numerous books and designed jackets and magazine covers. Although the subject matter of his work has been varied, he found the mathematical aspect of CIRCLES especially challenging to illustrate .

Mr. Giusti was born in Milan, Italy, and studied at the Royal Academy of Fine Arts of Brera there. He joined the faculty of the Famous Artists School International in Westport, Connecticut, and organized new courses in modern design.

Mr. Giusti lives in New York City and in West Redding, Connecticut, where he recently designed and built his contemporary house and studio.